STORYTELLING

by the same author

WELCOME TO THE DOLLHOUSE
HAPPINESS

STORYTELLING
Todd Solondz

faber and faber

First published in 2001
by Faber and Faber Limited
3 Queen Square London WC1N 3AU
Published in the United States by Faber and Faber Inc.
an affiliate of Farrar, Straus and Giroux LLC, New York

Photoset by Faber and Faber Ltd
Printed in England by Mackays of Chatham plc, Chatham, Kent

All rights reserved

© Todd Solondz, 2001
Photos pp. 5, 20, 22, 34, 41, 64 © New Line Prods., 2000
Photos pp. 7, 36, 48 © New Line Cinema, 2001
Photos pp. 11, 40, 52, 58, 61, 67 © Fine Line Features, 2001

The right of Todd Solondz to be identified as author of this work has
been asserted in accordance with Section 77 of the Copyright, Designs
and Patents Act 1988

This book is sold subject to the condition that it shall not, by way of trade or
otherwise, be lent, resold, hired out or otherwise circulated without the publisher's
prior consent in any form of binding or cover other than that in which it is
published and without a similar condition including this condition being imposed
on the subsequent purchaser

A CIP record for this book
is available from the British Library

ISBN 0–571–21283–2

For my Mom,
who has always been my favorite storyteller

CONTENTS

Unhappiness: an introduction by Bruce Wagner, ix

STORYTELLING, 1

UNHAPPINESS

Todd Solondz is a specialist who works in the broad field of human passion and human frailty – to put a finer point on it, he is a surgeon operating in a theater of contradictory acts: of class struggles, sexual ambiguity, everyday desires and ambitions, both aborted and perversely realized. Mr Solondz is continually arrested by the exorbitantly mundane actions and words that so often wound or poison. He exposes them in ways that are, of course, lively (even jaunty) but deadly too, for he is not a 'social observer,' at least not in the witty or worn or scintillating or pallid senses that phrase connotes; he isn't so much interested in foibles as he is in endgames. For him, the repercussions of betrayal, whether that betrayal be banal or remarkable, and the repercussions of words and acts, are final and heartbreaking, and become portals to the lower depths. So that is where we go, if willing and able; rewards await the accidental, fearless or inveterate traveler. Along the way there is danger, but there is always beauty and there is logic and there are tender sympathies in his grand tours. Those qualities prevail.

Storytelling is simply that: a title that, impossibly, says all. Mr Solondz is a conundrum. He is unusual in that his art presents itself in the simplest, most straightforward fashion, yet upon examination it is complex. The art and craft of this screenplay is more minimalist than in his prior movies, while at the same time being somehow more challenging. The film is divided into two parts: 'Fiction' and 'Nonfiction.' The 'Fiction' section is about college kids struggling to write short stories; the 'Nonfiction' section is about a filmmaker struggling with the idea of giving his documentary the fictionalized spin it may need in order to become a hit. At the end of 'Fiction,' a student who has been seduced by her teacher in a manner that some might interpret as degrading writes a heartfelt, literal story about that encounter and reads it aloud; her classmates promptly deride her efforts as racist, dishonest, phallocentric and, worst of all, 'unbelievable.' In 'Nonfiction,' the slacker subject of a documentary sullenly congratulates its director for having been mercenary enough to re-edit his life so that it would now be of interest to a paying (or, at least, cable-watching) public. In our times, we have experienced the death of fiction and the death of reality. Both sections that comprise Mr Solondz's film are 'too real,' as can be said of life, and of the best fiction too.

Storytelling is a hard film to watch. It is hilarious and it is sad, and gutsy and delicate, indelicate, violent, inviolate, unpredictable and *musical*, as are all of Mr Solondz's films. It has the mood and *chiaroscuro* of one of those Old Master portraits – students in an amphitheater gathered to observe a poorly anesthetized medical procedure – yet one finds it difficult to look away. At the end of his tale, one wonders, Where is there for Mr Solondz to go?

While I'm certain he would protest, *Storytelling* is a film so rigorous as to possess an unquestionable religiosity; all of his characters (he has said that once he casts an actor, that actor will never again be used unless reprising his original role) are transgressors, penitents, confessors and martyrs; there is grace in their longings and torments; there is a kind of shared, sacred acuity in watching them; and there is a gratitude for their existence. And so it is that this director's body of work will eventually be regarded as the 100 diaries of 100 country priests.

Bruce Wagner

Storytelling was first shown (in a slightly different cut) at the Cannes Film Festival in May 2001.

MAIN CAST
'Fiction'

VI	Selma Blair
MARCUS	Leo Fitzpatrick
MR SCOTT	Robert Wisdom
AMY	Maria Thayer
ELLI	Angela Goethals
LUCY	Devorah Rose
JOYCE	Nancy Anne Ridder
ETHAN	Steven Rosen
CATHERINE	Aleksa Palladino
MELINDA	Mary Lynn Rajskub
SUE	Tina Holmes

'Nonfiction'

TOBY OXMAN	Paul Giamatti
MIKE	Mike Schank
MR DEMARCO	Xander Berkeley
SCOOBY LIVINGSTON	Mark Webber
MARTY LIVINGSTON	John Goodman
FERN LIVINGSTON	Julie Hagerty
MIKEY LIVINGSTON	Jonathan Osser
BRADY LIVINGSTON	Noah Fleiss
CONSUELO	Lupe Ontiveros
CHERYL	Jessica Dunphy
ESPOSITO	Nick Maltes
MR KIRK	Steve Railsback
ELIZABETH ST. CLAIR	Crista Moore
TOBY'S EDITOR	Franka Potente
STANLEY	Andrew Marantz
CONAN O'BRIEN	Conan O'Brien

FOOTBALL COACH	Frederick Owens
DR BARRY JORDAN	Dr Barry Jordan
DR ROBIN GOODMAN	Dr Robin Goodman
DAVE	Eric Nieves
ONLOOKER #1	Marisa Redanty
ONLOOKER #2	Ilana Levine

MAIN CREW

Written and Directed by	Todd Solondz
Producers	Ted Hope
	Christine Vachon
Director of Photography	Frederick Elmes
Editor	Alan Oxman
Production Designer	James Chinlund
Costume Designer	John Dunn
Music	Belle & Sebastian
	Nathan Larson
Music Supervisor	Susan Jacobs
Line Producer	Declan Baldwin
Executive Producers	David Linde
	Amy Henkels
	Mike De Luca
Casting by	Ann Goulder

A Good Machine/Killer Films Production

TITLE CARD: *'Fiction'*

INT. MARCUS'S DORM ROOM – NIGHT

The time is circa 1985.

Vi and Marcus finish making love. Marcus has cerebral palsy.

> MARCUS
> Hey, you want to hear my short story now?

> VI
> Huh?

> MARCUS
> *(lifts a MS from a shelf by his bed)*
> I can read it to you.

> VI
> You mean, again?

> MARCUS
> Well, I changed the ending a little.

> VI
> Oh. What happens now?

> MARCUS
> Well, actually, it's the same, but longer. I think it's better. More . . . raw.

> VI
> Well then, maybe you should just read the ending.

> MARCUS
> But it won't make any sense if you hear it out of context.

> VI
> I think you should leave it the way it was. It was good.

Pause.

                      MARCUS
So you don't want to hear my new ending?

                      VI
You'll read it in class tomorrow. Surprise me.
                      (beat)
Anyway, I have to go. I promised Melinda I'd help her with her oral.

She rises, starts dressing.

                      MARCUS
You're tired of me. I can tell.

                      VI
Marcus, I'm tired. That's all.

                      MARCUS
You've lost interest . . . You hardly even sweat any more when we have sex.

                      VI
I was never much of a sweater. You know that.

                      MARCUS
Look, Vi, I don't blame you. You feel pity now. The pleasure isn't there any more. The kinkiness has gone . . . You've become kind.

EXT. CAMPUS GREEN – DAY

It is bright and sunny.

INT. MR SCOTT'S CLASSROOM – DAY

Mr Scott, who is black, presides over his class. Marcus is reading from his story, Vi at his side. Catherine, a stunning intellectual, sits near the teacher. The rest of the students (Amy, Elli, etc.) listen closely and take notes.

                      MARCUS
'. . . But when he saw *her* . . . it was as if he could walk like a

normal person. His legs didn't swing, his arms didn't spaz away . . . He wasn't a freak any more, for she made him forget his affliction. No more cerebral palsy! From now on "CP" stood for . . . cerebral person. He was a cerebral person.'

Pause. Marcus and Vi exchange looks.

AMY
I thought that was really good, Marcus . . . Really moving and emotional.

ELLI
Yeah, I thought it was really emotional, too.

AMY
And, I mean, really good word choices. It kind of reminded me a little of Faulkner, but East Coast and disabled.

LUCY
Or Flannery O'Connor. She had multiple sclerosis.

JOYCE
And Borges. He was blind.

Pause.

ETHAN
Updike has psoriasis.

Pause.

CATHERINE
Um . . . Maybe I'm wrong, but, um, I'm afraid I found the whole thing to be a little trite. Its earnestness is, well . . . it's a little embarrassing. And those adjectives, they're a little flat-footed. And redundant. I'm sorry, but . . . Anyway, what do I know? Don't even listen to what I say. I mean . . .

Pause.

MR SCOTT
Anyone else?

No response.

Catherine is right. The story's a piece of shit. You express nothing but banalities and, formally speaking, are unable to construct a single compelling sentence. You ride on a wave of clichés so worn, in fact, it actually approaches a level of grotesquerie. And your subtitle, 'the rawness of truth,' is that supposed to be a joke of some sort? Or are you just being pretentious?

(beat; then checking his class book)

OK. Who's next?

EXT. CAMPUS COURTYARD — DAY

Marcus, upset, rushes outside, Vi in pursuit, desperately trying to console.

VI

Marcus, wait up!

Marcus stops.

MARCUS

What do you want?

VI

Don't be so upset. It's OK . . .

MARCUS

What the fuck are you talking about? What's OK?

VI

(beat)

You know he hated my story also.

MARCUS

Your story was terrible!

He moves on, she keeps up with him.

VI

Marcus . . . You'll write something better next time!

MARCUS

Patronizing fuck! If you had just been honest with me in the first place I wouldn't have read it. *I* knew it was shit. But — idiot! — I believed you!

Marcus breaks up with Vi.

VI

That's not fair! I was honest! Just because I wasn't sucking up like that bitch Catherine.

MARCUS

Well, I sure didn't hear you voice your opinion in there when it mattered.

VI

I admit it – I was scared! I was shocked, in fact, by what he said. And he's so . . . convincing. I'm sorry if I let you down, but really, I still say he's just one opinion. I don't even like his books that much. They're all so . . . aggressively confrontational. I don't care if he's won the Pulitzer Prize.

Catherine and Mr Scott walk by together in the distance.

MARCUS

You just want to fuck him. Like Catherine and every other white cunt on campus.

He leaves her.

INT. VI AND MELINDA'S DORM ROOM — NIGHT

Melinda lies on her bed with some homework, watching Vi.

> VI (O.S.)
> (*on phone*)
> ... But, Marcus! You can't just unilaterally decide to end things. This is a relationship we're talking about! A friendship! You don't just ... Fuck you!

She hangs up and enters her bedroom, in tears.

> VI
> Fuck him! Fuck him! Fuck him! ...

> MELINDA
> Vi? Are you OK?

> VI
> Yes. I'm OK. I'm totally OK.

Melinda rises, puts a hand on her shoulder.

> MELINDA
> You did the right thing.

> VI
> I know that. Fucking cripple. Why do I waste my time with undergrads? They're all so ... juvenile! Uch! I just thought Marcus would be different. I mean, he's got CP!

Pause.

> MELINDA
> What are you gonna do now?

> VI
> I dunno ... go to a bar ... get laid ... whatever ... Don't worry about me. I'll be just fine ...

She starts changing into a new outfit.

EXT. BAR — NIGHT

Students hang around outside. Vi goes inside.

Vi needs a drink.

INT. BAR — NIGHT

Vi walks up to the bar.

VI

Can I have a beer?

After getting her beer, Vi turns around and suddenly notices Mr Scott, who is sitting alone. She goes over to him.

Hi.

MR SCOTT

Hello, Vi.

VI

What are you doing here?

MR SCOTT

What are you doing here?

VI

I'm sorry. I didn't mean . . . I mean, I just didn't expect to run into you here, that's all.

MR SCOTT

Well, now you have.

Vi laughs, sort of, then blushes.

VI

Yeah, um, then . . . are you alone?

MR SCOTT

Uh huh.

VI

Can I join you?

Mr Scott gestures for her to sit down with him.

Gee, thanks. Well, um . . . I just wanted to say that I'm really happy with the class and, um . . . I know you must hear this all the time, but I'm also a great admirer of your work. *A Sunday Lynching*, especially . . . really, um, spoke to me. God, I hope I'm not embarrassing you . . .

MR SCOTT

You're not.

VI

Good.

(*beat*)

'Cause I . . . um . . . I really agreed with everything you had to say last week about how bad my story was . . .

MR SCOTT

That's good.

VI

And I also agreed with what you said today about Marcus's story. It is a piece of shit.

Pause.

MR SCOTT

You have beautiful skin.

VI

Thank you.

(beat)
So Catherine seems like she might become a really good writer.

MR SCOTT

Maybe. She's OK.

Pause.

VI

Aren't you going out with Catherine?
(beat)
I'm sorry. It's none of my business. I didn't mean . . .

MR SCOTT

I'm not 'going out' with Catherine.

VI

Oh.
(beat)
Do you think I have potential as a writer?

MR SCOTT

No.

VI

Thank you for being honest.

Mr Scott leans over and touches her hand.

I have so much respect for you.

EXT. STREET – NIGHT

Mr Scott and Vi walk together in silence.

INT. MR SCOTT'S APARTMENT – NIGHT

Vi and Mr Scott enter. He turns around and looks at her. Pause.

VI

Can I just freshen up for a second?

He indicates the direction of the bathroom.

MR SCOTT

It's over there.

VI

Thanks.

INT. MR SCOTT'S BATHROOM – NIGHT

Vi enters, locks the door behind her. She looks at herself in the mirror, then notices a snapshot of Catherine: she is naked, legs opened wide. Other erotic photographs lie beneath Catherine's.

VI
(*to herself, almost chanting*)
Don't be racist. Don't be racist. Don't be racist . . .

INT. MR SCOTT'S BEDROOM – NIGHT

Vi emerges from the bathroom to find Mr Scott lounging on his bed.

VI

It's a really nice place you have. Is the rent high?

MR SCOTT

Take off your top.

She obliges.

Now . . . take off the rest.

She does, and he looks hard at her. Finally he rises.

Turn around.

She does.

Bend over.

He starts making love to her, from behind.

(*whispers*)
Say, 'Nigger, fuck me.'

VI

Oh, bu . . . uh . . . I can't say that.

'Take off your top.'

                        MR SCOTT

Say, Ni . . .

                        VI

Ni . . .

                        MR SCOTT

. . . gger.

                        VI

. . . gger.

                        MR SCOTT

Say, 'Nigger.'

                        VI

Nigger.

                        MR SCOTT

'Fuck me hard!'

                        VI

Fuck me hard!

                    MR SCOTT
Say, 'Nigger, fuck me hard!'

                    VI
Nigger, fuck me hard!

                    MR SCOTT
Again!

                    VI
Nigger, fuck me hard!! . . .

                    MR SCOTT
Again!!

                    VI
NIGGER, FUCK ME HARD!!! . . .

EXT. MARCUS'S DORMITORY – NIGHT

Lights are out.

INT. MARCUS'S DORM ROOM – NIGHT

Marcus looks in the mirror, ponders his reflection.

                    MARCUS
Freak.

There is a soft knock at the door. He turns away from the mirror and opens it. Vi is there, teary-eyed, disheveled.

                    VI
Can I come in?

They embrace.

                    MARCUS
You're all . . . sweaty!

INT. MR SCOTT'S CLASSROOM – DAY

Vi finishes reading her story to the class.

                    VI
'. . . So John flipped her around and slammed her against the

wall. Jane braced herself: she thought about her mother. She thought about Peter. She thought about God . . . and rape. "Say, 'Fuck me, nigger. Fuck me hard.'" John's flesh abraded her soft skin. There would be marks. She acquiesced, and said what he asked her to say, and did what he asked her to do. She had entered college with hope, with dignity, but she would graduate as a whore.'

Silence.

AMY
Why do people have to be so ugly . . . write about such ugly characters? It's perverted. I know you all think I'm being prissy, but I don't care. I was brought up in a certain way. And this is . . . mean-spirited!

Pause.

JOYCE
Yeah, well, it did seem a little affected. Like by using taboo language you were trying to shock us about the hollowness of your characters.

ETHAN
I think it was a little bit racist.

ELLI
It was completely racist, and beyond that I felt deeply offended as a woman. As if women can only operate from experiences of objectification.

SUE
Totally phallocentric.

ELLI
And so weirdly misogynistic. I mean, why does Jane go through with this? Is she stupid?

ETHAN
Hey, but wasn't this a rape? Or . . . did I miss something? Because I – I'm confused. Because if this was a rape, then why would she be a whore?

CATHERINE
(*beat*)

It was confessional, yet dishonest. Jane pretends to be horrified by the sexuality that she in fact fetishizes. She subsumes herself to the myth of black male sexual potency, but then doesn't follow through. She thinks she 'respects Afro-Americans,' she thinks they're 'cool,' 'exotic,' what a notch he'd make in her belt, but, of course, it all comes down to mandingo cliché, and he calls her on it. In classic racist tradition she demonizes, then runs for cover. But then, how could she behave otherwise? She's just a spoiled suburban white girl with a Benetton rainbow complex. It's just my opinion, and what do I know . . . but I think it's a callow piece of writing.

MR SCOTT

Callow and coy. Jane wants more, but isn't honest enough to admit it. In the end, she returns to the safety of her crippled (translation: sexually impotent) boyfriend.

MARCUS

This is bullshit! Her story was the truth!

JOYCE

Right.

SUE

It's unbelievable!

ELLI

It's clichéd!

AMY

It's disgusting!

VI

But it happened!

Silence.

MR SCOTT

I don't know about 'what happened,' Vi, because once you start writing, it all becomes fiction. Still, it certainly is an improvement over your last story: there is now at least a beginning, a middle, and an end.

TITLE CARD: *'Nonfiction'*

INT. TOBY'S BEDROOM – NIGHT

A Lower East Side tenement apartment. A Dogma '95 poster hangs above the bed.

Toby, down and out and in his thirties, leafs through his high-school yearbook. He reads an inscription: 'Toby, I just know you're going to become a movie star! Please don't forget me when you make it to the top! I will always love you – Pam.'

He picks up his phone and dials.

      PAM (V.O.)
Hello?

      TOBY
Hello, is this Pam?

      PAM (V.O.)
Who is this?

      TOBY
Toby Oxman.

      PAM (V.O.)
Toby –? Oh, hi! How are you?

      TOBY
Oh, fine. How are you?

      PAM (V.O.)
Great!

      TOBY
Great!

      PAM (V.O.)
So what's going on?

                              TOBY
That's what I was just gonna ask you.

                            PAM (V.O.)
But . . . you called.

                              TOBY
Oh, yeah, well . . . um . . . I was just calling because, well, I
was wondering if you still remembered me, which I guess
you do . . .

                            PAM (V.O.)
Yeah.

Pause.

                              TOBY
So. Look at where we are: the year 2000! Can you believe it?
I mean, did you ever think we would actually make it?

                            PAM (V.O.)
Um, well, yeah.
                            (*beat*)
So are you still acting?

                              TOBY
Oh, no, not any more. No, um, I kind of came to terms with
myself, I realized I had done what I had to do. And it was
time to move on.

                            PAM (V.O.)
Oh. So what did you do after you gave up on acting?

                              TOBY
Well, I went to law school, if you can believe that.

*Mike, Toby's roommate and cameraman, enters looking for a towel,
then goes to take a shower.*

                            PAM (V.O.)
I believe it.

                              TOBY
Yeah, well, it was really all kind of a joke – and a rip-off, so,
uh . . . so I dropped out.

PAM (V.O.)

Oh, that's too bad.

TOBY

Yeah, well, then it got me writing, so that was a good thing.

PAM (V.O.)

Anything I might know about?

TOBY

Well, um, I kind of let things go on this novel I'd been really into – I mean, the whole publishing industry is totally corrupt. I mean, really, it's finished.

PAM (V.O.)

That's too bad.

TOBY

I worked over at a homeless shelter for a while, drove a cab to pay the rent, but, I mean, that was like – I mean, I have some dignity.

PAM (V.O.)

That's good. So then what do you do now?

TOBY

I'm a documentary filmmaker.

PAM (V.O.)

Oh? Anything I might have seen?

TOBY

N-not yet. I'm hoping to get a grant for this one project on teenagers. Geez, remember when we were teenagers?

PAM (V.O.)

Yeah. You didn't wanna take me to the prom.

TOBY

Oh, I don't remember that . . .

PAM (V.O.)

I do.

                          TOBY
Well, but it was so long ago. We were so different back then . . .

No response.

Uh, well, anyway, so I'm looking for subjects for this documentary on teenage life in suburbia. Kind of an exploration of the psyche of its mythology. I wrote to Derrida to see if he'd like to do the narration. But everything's still kind of in development at this point.

                       PAM (V.O.)
Hunh.

                          TOBY
                        (*beat*)
I work in a shoe store right now. But it's cool. I'm not ashamed. I mean, really, I have a much stronger sense of self now. And, uh, anyway, it's really very temporary.

                       PAM (V.O.)
That's good.

                          TOBY
Yeah . . . um . . . so anyway, tell me. What about you? I'd heard through the grapevine you were producing movies.

                       PAM (V.O.)
Yeah. But not any more.

                          TOBY
Oh. Tired of 'life in the fast lane'?

No response.

Yeah . . . So you're um . . . you're married?

                       PAM (V.O.)
Yeah.

                          TOBY
Huh. Kids?

                       PAM (V.O.)
Yeah.

                    TOBY

How many?

                    PAM (V.O.)

Three.

                    TOBY

Great. How old are they?

                    PAM (V.O.)

Eight, six, and four.

                    TOBY

Wow, that really is great. In a few years, who knows, maybe they'll want to be in my documentary!

Pause.

                    PAM (V.O.)

Listen, Toby, I can't really talk right now. Do you mind if I call you back?

                    TOBY

Yeah, sure.

                    PAM (V.O.)

OK. Bye.

                    TOBY
              (*to himself, after a pause*)
Maybe she has caller ID.

EXT. FAIRFIELD HIGH SCHOOL — DAY

It is bright and sunny.

                    MR DEMARCO (V.O.)
Do you have any hobbies?

INT. MR DEMARCO'S OFFICE — DAY

Scooby, seventeen, and Mr DeMarco, the guidance counselor, sit opposite each other.

Scooby's school.

SCOOBY

No, not really.

MR DEMARCO

Any books you like to read for fun?

SCOOBY

No.

MR DEMARCO

None at all? How about those 'underground' comics?

SCOOBY

I hate reading.

MR DEMARCO
(*beat*)

All right, Scooby, let's not beat around the bush. With your attitude, you're not going to get in anywhere.

SCOOBY

OK.

MR DEMARCO
'OK.' So you just don't care.
(*beat*)
Let me ask you, not as your guidance counselor, but . . . as a friend: what do you want to do with your life? I mean, what kind of long-term goals can you possibly have?

SCOOBY
I dunno . . .

MR DEMARCO
C'mon. Talk to me. Tell me what you're thinking.

SCOOBY
Well, I mean . . . I wanna be on TV. Maybe have a talk show or something. Like Conan. Or early Letterman.

MR DEMARCO
Ah-hah. And how is it you hope to achieve this goal?

SCOOBY
I dunno. See if I have any connections.

EXT. LIVINGSTON HOME – EVENING

The sprinkler system is still on.

INT. DINING ROOM – EVENING

The family is sitting waiting at the table: Fern, Scooby's attractive mother; Marty, his bullish father; Brady, sixteen, his handsome jock brother; and Mikey, ten, his smart youngest brother.

Consuelo, the maid, brings some bread to the table.

FERN
Did you knock on his door?

MIKEY
Yes, but he just shouted at me and used the f-word.

MARTY
Scooby! Dinner!

No response. Pause.

Fern is concerned about Scooby.

MIKEY
Would anyone be interested in being hypnotized after dinner?

FERN/MARTY/BRADY
No.

Pause.

FERN
Let's just start.

They eat.

MARTY
I don't know what's wrong with that kid.

BRADY
Maybe he's gay.

MARTY
Don't ever say that.

BRADY
What if he is?

MARTY
He isn't.

FERN
Marty, ignore him.

BRADY
He's vegetarian, doesn't do sports . . .

MARTY
Brady!

Pause.

FERN
And even if he is . . .

Pause.

MIKEY
Gay people are people too, you know. You're just being prejudiced.

BRADY

I don't care if he's gay. I'm cool. I mean, it's not like I have to share his room or anything.

MARTY

I just want to know what the hell he's doing in his room that's so interesting he doesn't come down for dinner.

MIKEY

Maybe he's building a bomb . . . just like –!

FERN

Don't even joke about that!

MIKEY

I'm serious! What happens if he blows up the school?

A tense pause, followed by a distant crashing sound.

SCOOBY (O.S.)

Fuck!

MARTY

I'm going in there.

Scooby appears.

SCOOBY

Was anyone in my room today?

FERN

Is everything OK?

SCOOBY

My CD case like totally collapsed. I'm gonna have to recatalogue all weekend.
  (*sitting down*)
Hey. Can you pass the salad over?

MARTY
  (*beat*)
Steak's really good tonight.

SCOOBY
(*beat*)

Good.

FERN

Got a lot of homework?

SCOOBY

I dunno.

MARTY

Whaddya mean you don't know? You either got a lot or you don't. What's not to know?

FERN

Marty . . .

MARTY
(*beat*)

You started filling out your college applications yet?

SCOOBY

I'm not going to college.

Pause.

FERN

What are you going to do?

SCOOBY

I dunno.

MARTY

What *do* you know?

SCOOBY

Dad, I'm trying to figure things out right now, OK? It's like, really hard, and I'm just listening to some old Elton John and . . .

Brady mouths: 'Gay!'

MARTY

Out! Leave the table!

BRADY

What?

MARTY

You heard me: leave the table!

BRADY
(*rising*)

Man, I am out of here! This family is so fucked!

Brady leaves.

MIKEY

Mom, it's not fair if Brady can say the f-word and I can't.

MARTY

Yeah, well, Mikey, listen up. 'Cause here's a lesson: life's not fair.

EXT. LIVINGSTON HOME — DAY

A red sports car drives up front. Esposito, Brady's buddy, drops off Brady and Cheryl, Brady's cheerleader girlfriend.

A cleaning woman walks along the sidewalk on her way to the bus stop.

BRADY

I'll talk to you later, man!

ESPOSITO

Yo, dude!

CHERYL

Thanks, Esposito!

INT. TV ROOM — DAY

Brady, still in his football outfit, tracks in some dirt. Cheryl follows him to his room, giggling.

Mikey sits on the sofa while Consuelo continues her housework.

MIKEY

Consuelo?

CONSUELO

Yes, Mikey?

MIKEY

Do you have any brothers or sisters?

CONSUELO

Yes.

MIKEY

Really? How many?

CONSUELO

Four brothers and five sisters.

MIKEY

Wow.

(*beat*)

Why did your parents have so many children? I mean, if they were poor, wouldn't it be better to have just one or two?

CONSUELO

It was God's will.

MIKEY

But do you really believe in God? And heaven, hell and angels and all that kind of stuff?

CONSUELO

(*beat*)

No.

INT. DINING ROOM — EVENING

The Livingstons are eating dinner.

MARTY

So? How was school today?

SCOOBY

The same.

MARTY

The same. Same as what?

SCOOBY

Just the same.

A tense pause.

BRADY

We're studying the Holocaust in Social Studies.

MARTY

Oh, yeah?

SCOOBY

We did the same thing last year also.

FERN

How was the class?

BRADY

Well, I'm supposed to watch *Schindler's List* for homework. The movie's like almost four hours. And then I'm supposed to write a report on survivors.
(*to Marty*)
You know any survivors, Dad?

MARTY

Hmmm . . . Do I know any . . . personally . . . ?

FERN

Well, technically your Zeda is a survivor.

BRADY

He was in a concentration camp?

FERN

Well, no. But he had to escape the Nazis.

BRADY

But I thought he came over to America before the war.

FERN

Well, he did. With his family. But his cousins, they had to stay and they were all killed. And if he'd stayed, he would have been killed. So in my book he's a survivor.

BRADY
Even though it was only his cousins that were killed?

FERN
But that could've happened to *him*. Or to me, if I'd been alive. Or you.

MIKEY
Or me?

SCOOBY
You mean, then, we're all survivors?

FERN
Well . . . yes. If it hadn't been for Hitler, he wouldn't have had to leave Europe. We would have been . . . European.

SCOOBY
But then, in a sense, since you would never have met Dad if your family had stayed in Europe . . . if it weren't for Hitler, none of us would have been born.

A long pause.

MARTY
Get the hell outta here!

SCOOBY
(*rising*)
Man, it's just, like, conversation.

INT. PRINCIPAL'S OFFICE – DAY

Toby sits across from Mr Kirk.

MR KIRK
Tell me: you make a living at this?

TOBY
Well, sir . . . uh . . . I'm actually not doing this for the money. When you make a documentary, you do it for many reasons, but money is certainly not one of them.

MR KIRK
I don't get it.

                              TOBY

Well, sir, a lot has happened to the landscape of the suburban high school since I was a student, and I feel it would be a valuable, perhaps even enlightening endeavour, to chronicle the changes, to get intimate with the realities kids and parents face in American schools today.

Pause.

                              MR KIRK

Yeah, well, whatever. I'll let you know if there's interest.

INT. HALLWAY — DAY

Toby pauses by the receptionist before leaving.

                              TOBY

Excuse me, where's the bathroom?

INT. LAVATORY — DAY

Toby rushes to the urinal. Scooby is sitting in a corner, smoking a joint, observing him. Toby smells the pot, turns and smiles at him.

                              SCOOBY

You a pervert?

                              TOBY

No . . . Actually, I'm a documentary filmmaker.

                              SCOOBY

Oh. You mean, like, *Blair Witch Project*?

                              TOBY

Well, no. I'm doing one on high-school students, in fact.

                              SCOOBY

What for?

                              TOBY

Well . . . it's kind of a sociological study in the aftermath of Columbine.

                              SCOOBY

Is this to like get into Sundance?

TOBY
Yeah, well, it's possible they would be interested in it.

SCOOBY
Doubt it.

TOBY
Actually, there is some interest from the Sundance Channel.

SCOOBY
Whoopee.

TOBY
HBO and MTV have also shown some interest.

Pause.

SCOOBY
So you have connections . . .

EXT. LIVINGSTON HOME – NIGHT

The lights are on.

TOBY (V.O.)
You see, we're trying to do a film on suburban lifestyles . . .

INT. LIVINGSTON HOME – NIGHT

Toby sits in the living room surrounded by the Livingston family.

Marty fingers a card that reads: TOBY OXMAN, DOCUMENTARIAN. *His address and phone number are printed below.*

TOBY
. . . kind of *An American Family* for the new millennium . . .

FERN
I thought this was about kids getting into college.

TOBY
Oh, it is. I mean –

MARTY
Which is it? You gotta keep your focus straight.

TOBY

You're absolutely right. The focus is on the college admissions process today.

Pause.

MARTY

And you want Scooby to be the focus of all this.

TOBY

Scooby and a few other students of different socioeconomic backgrounds.

MARTY

You didn't mention any other students before.

TOBY

Oh, well, I don't have them yet, but –

MARTY

Either Scooby is the focus, or forget it.

SCOOBY

Yeah, I thought I was the focus.

MIKEY

I wanna be the focus.

Brady slaps him.

FERN

Toby, we need this to be a positive experience.

TOBY

Well, I suppose I could reconceive . . .

MARTY

Reconceive.

TOBY

'Cause Scooby does have a quality that I've been looking for, a quality that is emblematic of America today. It's part disillusionment, part hope . . .

Consuelo comes in with tea and Twinkies.

                                MIKEY

Twinkies!

                                FERN

Boys, take napkins . . . Napkins . . .

                                MARTY

Not to be crass, but what do we get out of this?

                                FERN
                              (*laughs*)
Don't worry, he doesn't mean money.

                                TOBY

Oh, I know, I know that. Well, sharing your story, your ups
and downs, and so forth, can, I hope, be an illuminating
experience.

                                MARTY

Yeah . . . How do we know we won't be exploited?

                                FERN

No, it's true.

                                TOBY

Mr Livingston, I fully understand and I share your concerns.
You feel vulnerable. And I know that this is a very difficult
question, but what it comes down to is: can you make a leap
of faith in me, in the same way that I have to make a leap of
faith in you?

ON VIDEO: INT. LOCKER ROOM – DAY

Big Esposito, in football attire, surrounded by Brady and other athletes, talks to Toby. Kids whip towels at each other in the background.

                              ESPOSITO

This is a great school. I don't care what anybody says. I
mean, it's not perfect, but like the people are really cool, like
the teachers and kids . . . they really care and all. And I know
that they make fun of New Jersey all the time, but I don't
care. 'Cause they're just snobs. 'Cause Jersey is where America's at!

'Can you make a leap of faith in me . . .?'

ON VIDEO: INT. EMPTY SCHOOL HALLWAY – DAY

                  TOBY (V.O.)

Walking down these hallways, hallways just like the ones I once walked down as a teenager, I couldn't help thinking back to a time when every day I woke up depressed, suicidal, consumed by despair. Had things changed? Was the competition to get into the most prestigious schools still a requisite rite of passage? Beneath these masks of courtesy and friendliness I knew that there were darker forces at work . . . and I knew that Scooby was the key to revealing the truth . . .

VARIOUS SHOTS OF SCOOBY

. . . looking pensive.

                  TOBY (V.O.)

Scooby, Scooby, Scooby . . . What are you thinking? College, SATs, your parents, your brothers, your friends . . . How is it you deal with all this stress?

ON VIDEO: INT. CLASSROOM — DAY

A school psychologist sits at her desk.

> ELIZABETH ST. CLAIR
> The pressure to get into the college of your choice is incredible. You know, they did a study recently of the youth in Bosnia during the bombing, and they found that the stress the young people experienced there was less than what American high-school students go through when applying to college.

> TOBY (O.S.)
> Is that right?

> ELIZABETH ST. CLAIR
> Yes.

> TOBY (O.S.)
> Oh, my God . . .

INT. EDITING ROOM — NIGHT

Toby and his Editor examine the footage on an AVID.

> TOBY
> So whaddya think?

> EDITOR
> Well, I'm not really sure what you're trying to say. It's funny, I suppose. But it seems glib and facile to just make fun of how idiotic these people are.

> TOBY
> I'm not making fun. I'm showing it as it really is.

> EDITOR
> You're showing how superior you are to your subject.

> TOBY
> No, but I like my subject. I like these people.

> EDITOR
> No, you don't.

Toby's editor critiques his work.

TOBY

Yes, I do. I love them!

Pause.

EDITOR

The camerawork's nice.

TOBY

Thanks. I'll tell Mike.
        (beat)
Well, it's still just a beginning. I know I can . . . dig deeper.

EXT. LIVINGSTON HOME – DAY

It is bright and sunny.

INT. LIVINGSTON HOME – DAY

Fern is in the kitchen talking on the phone. She has a list of names and notes in front of her. Consuelo dusts in the background.

Toby and Mike stand nearby with a video camera, recording everything.

FERN

. . . but Marj – may I call you Marj? – what it really boils down to is . . . what does it mean to be a Jew? . . . Exactly. Tzedakah. Charity. And the new wing at Beth Israel is . . . Well, actually, last year you gave $500. But this year $1,000 would not only be a mitzvah, it would bring you to a new level . . . Yes, of course. Your gift would also give you a Chagall menorah and two tickets to the dinner dance this spring . . . Because it's true: Israel needs us now. If not now, when? . . . Well, that's wonderful . . . I'll speak to you next week . . . You too! Take care!

She hangs up just as Scooby walks inside, fresh from school.

Hi, Scooby! How was school today?

SCOOBY

Fine.

FERN

Ready for tomorrow?

SCOOBY

What's tomorrow?

FERN

The SATs, knucklehead.

SCOOBY

I'm not taking them.

He walks off.

ON VIDEO: INT. DINING ROOM – EVENING

The family is eating dinner. There is a tense silence, finally broken by Mikey.

MIKEY

Mom?

FERN

Yes, Mikey?

MIKEY

I was looking through Scooby's SAT practice books this afternoon and I took one of the practice tests. Guess what score I got?

FERN

What?

MIKEY

550 verbal, 520 math. And I'm only in fifth grade!

Everyone turns to glare at him.

INT. CHILDREN'S BATHROOM – NIGHT

Scooby is brushing his teeth when Marty enters.

MARTY

Scooby?

                    SCOOBY
Yeah.

                    MARTY
We have to talk.

Pause.

                    SCOOBY
Whaddya wanna talk about?

                    MARTY
Don't screw around with me. You know what I'm talking about.
                    (*beat*)
You're taking those SATs. You're taking those SATs or your CD collection is history. You're taking those SATs and you're going to college. You're taking those SATs if I have to strap your ass to a chair, but buddy, you're taking them.

Pause.

                    SCOOBY
OK.

                    MARTY
          (*under his breath as he starts walking out*)
Tired of this shit . . .

INT. SCHOOL GYM – DAY

Toby and Mike shoot footage of the students as they take their SATs.

Scooby is filling out his SAT in such a way that he creates a pattern of filled blanks that spells: FUCK THIS SHIT.

EXT. LIVINGSTON HOME – DAY

Toby and Mike are interviewing Brady and Cheryl in the driveway. Off to the side, Mikey tries hypnotizing a cat.

                    TOBY
So are you surprised that Scooby took the SATs after all?

Shooting Scooby as he takes his SATs.

BRADY
Not really. He's kind of a wuss.

TOBY
OK. How about you, Cheryl? Were you surprised?

CHERYL
I dunno. Whatever.

TOBY
Hmm.

BRADY
Hey, how come you drive such a shitty car?

CHERYL
Yeah.

TOBY
(joins their laughter)
I don't know . . . That's interesting, though. A cool car. Is that something that's real important to you, Brady?

'Hey, how come you drive such a shitty car?'

                    BRADY
Yeah.

                    CHERYL
Uh duh.

INT. SCOOBY'S BEDROOM – DAY

Scooby handles a gun his friend Stanley has given him.

                    SCOOBY
Pretty cool, Stanley.

                    STANLEY
Thanks.

                    SCOOBY
How'd you get it?

                    STANLEY
It's my Dad's. He hides it under some old *TV Guides* in his closet.

SCOOBY

Gee, your Dad's smart.

STANLEY

I know.

SCOOBY

Is it loaded?

STANLEY

No, I don't think so . . .

Scooby points it at his head.

Scooby, don't! Be careful!

SCOOBY

I'm not an idiot, man. I watch TV.

STANLEY

I know. I'm sorry. I'm just . . . a little nervous, I don't know why.

SCOOBY

You should be.

Scooby points it at Stanley, gets a terrified reaction, then tosses the gun aside.

Here. You can keep it.

He lies down. Pause.

STANLEY

Scooby?

SCOOBY

Yeah?

STANLEY

You know . . . I like you.

SCOOBY

Yeah. I know.

STANLEY

I mean . . .

SCOOBY

I know. Everyone knows.

STANLEY

Oh.
(*beat*)
Do you think that you'd let me . . . um . . .

Pause.

SCOOBY

OK. If you feel like it. Just give me a second.

He pulls a bag of mushrooms out from beneath his night table, takes some and offers to Stanley.

You want some?

STANLEY

No, thanks.

Scooby flicks on a CD, then lies down.

DREAM SEQUENCE — EXT. LIVINGSTON HOME — DAY

While Stanley goes down on Scooby, the camera pans away from Scooby to reveal Marty and Fern being burned at the stake in the front yard, writhing and screaming in agony.

MARTY

I'm so sorry! I should never have made you take the SATs!

The camera then pans to reveal Conan O'Brien approaching.

CONAN

Hey, Scooby! How's it going?

SCOOBY

Conan O'Brien? Woah! What are you doing here?

CONAN

I'm looking for a last-minute guest for my show. Any suggestions?

SCOOBY

I'll be your guest!

CONAN
Really? Well, all right! Let's take a look at the television and see how we look.

The camera pans to reveal a TV standing on the lawn.

SCOOBY
Cool!

Conan turns on the TV and we move inside it to see Conan and Scooby sharing some talk-show patter and repartee.

CONAN
Welcome to the show, Scooby.

SCOOBY
Thank you.

CONAN
Nice to have you here.

SCOOBY
Great to be here.

CONAN
And thank you for dressing up for us. This is very classy. Tell us. What kind of professional plans do you have? What's in your future?

SCOOBY
Well, I was thinking . . . I might work for you.

CONAN
Ahh . . . tell me. What do you want to do for me? What's your idea?

SCOOBY
Be your sidekick, you know, and maybe eventually become a TV talk-show host.

CONAN
TV talk-show host, OK. You were at sidekick eight seconds ago, then TV talk-show host. You'll be a Latin dictator in about a minute.

Audience laughter.

> Let's see what they think of the first idea. I'm curious what the audience thinks. Folks, what do you think: should Scooby be my new sidekick?

Audience cheers.

> Scooby, new sidekick, everybody!

Bigger round of applause.

RETURN TO REALITY: INT. CHILDREN'S BATHROOM – NIGHT

Scooby has spaced out while flossing. There is a knock at the door.

SCOOBY

Yeah?

Brady enters.

BRADY

Hey.

SCOOBY

Hey. What's up?

BRADY

There's something I need to talk about with you.

SCOOBY

What?

BRADY

There are some rumors . . .

SCOOBY

Like what?

BRADY

You know . . . Stanley . . .

SCOOBY

Oh.

BRADY

And like, don't take this the wrong way . . . I mean, I'm cool

... but ... you know ... I've got a good reputation at school and, well ... I really don't want it ruined.

He is visibly upset. Pause.

                    SCOOBY

No prob. I'm cool.

                    BRADY

Thanks, Scoob.

EXT. HIGH-SCHOOL PLAYING FIELD — DAY

A football scrimmage is in progress. A play ends, and the Coach comes on to the field, barking:

                    COACH

Esposito, what the fuck do you think you're doing? You're tackling like a bitch on my football team, son! You gotta bend your ass over and hit somebody! You understand me?

                    ESPOSITO

Yes, sir!

                    COACH

You understand me?

                    ESPOSITO

Yes, sir!

                    COACH

Then do it! ... Livingston! That's the way to hit that hole, son!

Brady waves at Cheryl in the stands.

We're gonna become a football team today, guys! Let's move the ball! Move! Move! Move! I wanna see you hit those holes! Defense, fill those goddam gaps! Let's go, guys! Let's do it! ...

On the next play Brady runs to catch a pass, but is mowed down by Esposito shouting, 'KILL HIM!!!'

Cheryl jumps up, alarmed.

O.S. cheerleaders finish their 'Go Bucks!' cheer, but Brady doesn't rise.

INT. HOSPITAL CORRIDOR – DAY

Brady is rushed on a gurney into an operating room. Cheryl follows him as far as she can.

INT. HOSPITAL ICU – EVENING

Brady lies unconscious in bed, hooked up to machines. Marty, Fern, Scooby, and Cheryl stand around him.

INT. LIVINGSTON HOME – NIGHT

Mikey sits at the kitchen table with Consuelo. He is eating ice cream.

MIKEY
When I'm in high school I'm not going to play any football. I'm just going to concentrate on class rank.
(*beat*)
What did you do in high school?

CONSUELO
I did not go to high school.

MIKEY
Weren't there high schools in El Salvador?

CONSUELO
We had to work. My family was poor.

MIKEY
Must've been hard being poor.

CONSUELO
I'm still poor.

MIKEY
Hmmm.
(*beat*)
But, Consuelo, even though you're poor, don't you have any hobbies or interests or anything?

CONSUELO
No, Mikey.

Consuelo listens to Mikey's advice.

MIKEY
But like, what do you like to do when you're not working?

CONSUELO
I'm always working.

MIKEY
But when you're not. Like now. What do you like to do?

CONSUELO
This is work.

MIKEY
But it's not like real work. This is just babysitting.

Consuelo stares hard at him in silence.

You know, *your* job's really not so bad, if you think about it. You should smile more.

ON VIDEO: DOCUMENTARY FOOTAGE OF:

(1) Driving-along-the-neighborhood shots; a lamp post; a sign; a floating straw wrapper.

TOBY (V.O.)
When the sky is clear and the sun is warm, you're reminded of how beautiful things can be: a lamp post, a sign, a straw wrapper blowing in the wind . . . But when that dark cloud appears, you realize how fragile the balance of life is.

(2) The neurologist Dr Barry Jordan discussing Brady's condition:

DR JORDAN
When Brady first arrived at the hospital he was unresponsive to verbal stimuli. We performed a CT scan which demonstrated a large subdural hemotoma with mass effect. Since the removal of the subdural he's been in coma.

(3) A psychologist discussing the effect of the Brady crisis on his family:

DR GOODMAN
When I first met the Livingstons it was in the first twenty-four hours of Brady coming in after his tragic football accident and they were acting in a fairly typical way . . .

(4) The Livingstons consulting with Dr Goodman in a hospital waiting room:

MARTY

We're not the ones who need the help. My son needs help.

DR GOODMAN

And you –

MARTY

My son's in there! He can't even feed himself, he can't eat – I don't even know if he's going to be a vegetable or not, for Chrissake!

The picture freezes and then zooms into a close-up on Scooby.

TOBY (V.O.)

But what about Scooby? How would this effect him? What meaning is to be found in this?

INT. EDITING ROOM – DAY

Toby and his Editor finish watching this latest footage.

EDITOR

This is definitely better.

TOBY

You think so? You don't think that this might not be a little dry?

EDITOR

This is not an entertainment you're making, Toby. This story about a kid in the suburbs and the state of the college admissions process has, with this Brady crisis, evolved into something much richer and more provocative.

TOBY

Yes, I know . . . But still, it should be somewhat entertaining.

EDITOR

I mean, without this footage, without this rigorous documentation, it would feel like exploitation.

TOBY

No, no, no. No exploitation. This is serious . . . But don't you find it a little funny too, at the same time?

EDITOR

You've got a family tragedy on your hands. Will you tell me what's funny about that? About a kid in a coma?

TOBY

Nothing, I guess . . .

EDITOR

I mean, why are you making this documentary if you can't treat your subject with appropriate gravity?

TOBY

OK, you're right, you're right . . .
(*beat*)
You know, we need to screen what we've got . . . invite some regular people, just some random off-the-street types . . . and see what real people think of this.

EDITOR

I dunno, Toby. We really have a long way to go. You still need a lot more footage, and it's probably a little premature to start screening . . .

TOBY

OK, then we can invite serious intellectual types.

EDITOR

We're not ready.

TOBY

Hip alternative types who will understand the process better . . .

EDITOR

We are not ready!

TOBY

Well, I need to see this with an audience!

EDITOR

What's an audience going to tell you?

                                TOBY
    I dunno. Maybe they'll like it.

INT. LIVINGSTON HOME — NIGHT

Mikey opens the refrigerator, takes out a bottle of grape juice, pours a cup for himself, then accidentally spills it all on the floor.

                               MIKEY
    Consuelo! I spilled some grape juice on the floor! . . . Consuelo?!

INT. BASEMENT RECREATION ROOM — NIGHT

Mikey goes downstairs, finds her alone in her bedroom. She appears to be upset.

                               MIKEY
    Consuelo?

No response.

    Consuelo. Are you crying?

Mikey calls Consuelo for help.

CONSUELO

No.

MIKEY

Yes, you are. I can tell. What's the matter?

CONSUELO

Mi Jesus . . . mi Jesus . . .

MIKEY

Speak English.

CONSUELO

Mi Jesus esta muerto!

MIKEY

Consuelo, I'm sorry, but you know if you don't speak English I can't understand you.

CONSUELO

My Jesus . . .

MIKEY

Who is Jesus?

CONSUELO

My baby.

MIKEY

You have a baby?

CONSUELO

My grandchild-baby.

MIKEY

Gee, I didn't even know you had any children. But why are you so upset about Jesus?

CONSUELO

He is dead.

MIKEY

Oh. How did that happen?

CONSUELO

He was executed. He was on Death Row and then he was executed.

MIKEY

How did they execute him?

CONSUELO

Poison gas.

MIKEY
(*beat*)

Maybe it's for the best . . . I mean, if he was guilty of doing something wrong . . . People who are bad should be killed. Don't you think so?

CONSUELO

Jesus was not bad.

MIKEY

Maybe he was and you just didn't know it.

CONSUELO

He wasn't.

MIKEY

But still, you can't be sure.

CONSUELO

I am sure.

MIKEY

But really, you never know.

CONSUELO

I know!

MIKEY
(*beat*)

Why was he on Death Row?

CONSUELO

For rape and murder.

Pause.

MIKEY
Consuelo, what is rape exactly?

CONSUELO
(*beat*)
It is when you love someone, and they don't love you. And then you do something about it.

Pause.

MIKEY
Sometimes I feel like my parents don't love me.

CONSUELO
Well then, when you get older you can do something about it.

A long pause.

MIKEY
Consuelo? I spilled some grape juice upstairs. Do you think you could clean up the floor now?

INT. BRADY'S BEDROOM – EVENING

Marty and Mikey sit by the comatose Brady, who lies now in his own bed.

MIKEY
Dad? . . . Do you think that Brady will ever get better?

MARTY
One in a million recover.

MIKEY
Maybe he's that one in a million!

MARTY
Mikey, there's optimism, and then there's stupidity. It's a very fine line.

Pause.

MIKEY
I don't think there's any hope, either. I was just trying to make you feel better.

                         MARTY

Thanks.

                         MIKEY

You're welcome.
                         (*beat*)
Dad? . . . Would you let me try hypnotizing you now?

                         MARTY

Yeah. Sure. Go ahead. Hypnotize me.

                         MIKEY

OK. Stay there. I'll be right back.

Mikey hurries off to fetch his hypnotizing apparatus. Marty sits and waits.

Just a sec! . . . Be right there!

Mikey returns, sets himself up across from Marty and takes out a shiny object.

Dad, can you turn around a bit, please?

Marty obliges.

Thanks. All right. Now you must look at this shiny object and concentrate. Relax your legs. Relax your arms. Relax your shoulders. Now keep your eyes on the shiny object . . . Your eyelids are getting heavy . . . heavier . . . You're getting sleepy . . . sleepier . . . Now let your eyes close shut . . . and you are sound asleep.

Marty's head drops.

Now you are completely under my power. I am the only voice you can hear, the only voice you will listen to. Now. When you wake up you will be in a good mood. You won't worry so much about Brady. And I will be your favorite from now on. If Brady dies, you can be sad for a little bit, but I will still be the most important person in your life. You will never be mean to me, and always give me whatever I want. Also, you should fire Consuelo. She's lazy. Now when I snap my fingers, you will remember nothing, but you will do everything I have asked. One. Two. Three.

Mikey snaps his fingers and Marty wakes up.

> MARTY
> Hey, Mikey. You wanna get some ice cream?

> MIKEY
> OK!

EXT. LIVINGSTON HOME — DAY

A couple of maids are walking by with white babies in strollers.

ON VIDEO: INT. SCOOBY'S BEDROOM — DAY

> SCOOBY
> So like, yeah . . . I caved in. I mean, I had to. My parents, they're like . . . still really depressed about Brady. So I wrote the bullshit essay. Filled out the applications, did the interviews . . . Y'know, I figure I can always drop out.

> TOBY (O.S.)
> So where'd you get in?

> SCOOBY
> Princeton.

> TOBY (O.S.)
> *(beat)*
> But what did you get on your SATs?

> SCOOBY
> 200 verbal/710 math. Kinda weird, I know. But I think they thought it was, like, good-weird.

ON VIDEO: INT. LIVING ROOM — EVENING

Marty and Fern sit on the sofa.

> MARTY
> We used pull.

Scooby tells Toby he got into Princeton.

                              FERN
You know, you have to. Sometimes you just have to, Toby.

                          TOBY (O.S.)
But what kind of pull did you have?

                              MARTY
I have a cousin. Very big giver to the alumni fund.

                              FERN
It's all about who you know.

                              MARTY
Look, we're not suckers. Everyone else is out there doing the same thing.

                              FERN
He's right.

EXT. LIVINGSTON HOME – DAY

Scooby watches Toby and Mike as they try fixing their jammed camera.

                              MIKE
Damn, Toby . . . This thing won't open again.

                              TOBY
Let me try it, let me try it.
            (*takes the camera from Mike*)
It's um . . . The button is just stuck.

                             SCOOBY
Hey, um, Toby? I was wondering . . . Is the documentary almost finished?

                              TOBY
Uh, yeah, we're getting there.

                             SCOOBY
Can I see what you have so far?

                              TOBY
Sure . . . um . . . yeah, as soon as I have a screening I'll let you know.

SCOOBY

Thanks, man.

INT. LIVINGSTON HOME — DAY

Mikey and Consuelo are playing cards.

MIKEY

Gin! I win! Let's play again!

He starts dealing another round when Marty suddenly appears, back from work.

MARTY

Hey, Mikey!

MIKEY

Hi, Dad!

MARTY

Come here, give me a hug!

MIKEY

Gee, you're home early!

MARTY

Yeah, uh, listen. Why don't you go upstairs and keep your Mom and Brady company for a bit? I need to speak alone with Consuelo for a moment.

MIKEY

Sure, Dad.

He runs up the stairs, pretends to disappear, but stays to observe.

MARTY

Consuelo. Mrs Livingston and I have discussed this, and we've come to the conclusion that we are not very happy with your work lately, so we're going to let you go.

CONSUELO

I – I don't understand.

MARTY

We've been happy with you in the past, but now we think

maybe it's time for a change . . . uh . . . I know you've had trouble at home and maybe, you know, some of that is reflected in your work . . .

CONSUELO
But, Mr Livingston, I work very hard for you and your family!

MARTY
I understand, I understand that, and I'm sorry. I'm sorry it had to end this way.

EXT. LIVINGSTON HOME – DAY

Consuelo exits the house and trudges towards the bus stop, carrying all her belongings. Other cleaning women are waiting for the bus as well.

INT. SCOOBY'S BEDROOM – DAY

Scooby is looking at the address on Toby's 'documentarian' calling card. He picks up the phone and dials.

Consuelo is fired.

INT. SHOE STORE — DAY

Dave, the store manager, leaves a customer for a moment to pick up the phone.

DAVE

Florsheim. Can I help you?

SCOOBY (V.O.)

Hi. I . . . uh . . . I'm trying to reach Toby Oxman?

DAVE

Sorry, he's off today.

BACK TO SCOOBY

. . . on the phone.

SCOOBY

OK . . . um . . . Thanks.

He hangs up.

EXT. HIGHWAY — DAY

Scooby drives his Mom's shiny new SUV to New York.

EXT. A RUN-DOWN TENEMENT NEIGHBORHOOD — DAY

Scooby pulls into a spot.

INT. TOBY'S APARTMENT BUILDING — DAY

Scooby climbs a stairwell, rings a bell. Mike opens the door.

SCOOBY

Hey, uh, Mike. Is Toby here?

MIKE

Uh, no, he's not.

SCOOBY

Oh. Do you have any idea where he might be?

MIKE

I think he's at a test screening.

EXT. TOBY'S APARTMENT BUILDING – DAY

Scooby hurries outside only to find his car stolen.

INT. SUBWAY – DAY

Scooby rides a train.

INT. SCREENING-ROOM FACILITY – DAY

Scooby sees a sign that reads: 'American Scooby: test screening.' He goes into the screening room.

SCOOBY'S POV

. . . of the documentary being screened.

ON VIDEO: EXT. LIVINGSTON HOME BACKYARD – DAY

Marty talks to Toby poolside as he prepares a barbecue.

MARTY
I think Scooby's like a lot of kids. He just hit a . . . a speed bump. Now he's gonna find his way, his path is gonna be cleared, and I think he's gonna continue his education at a good college. And everybody else is gonna be happy.

TOBY (O.S.)
. . . But Mr Livingston, aren't you a bit fearful that Scooby will be confronted with hollow values and systemic conformism?

Pause.

MARTY
I don't know why this is so hard for you to comprehend. I had a terrific time in college. I've got a terrific job, a comfortable salary, terrific wife, three terrific kids . . . and every year I give to the alumni fund. Now why are you trying to make college out to be a bad thing, a negative experience? You were unhappy? Well, too bad! Get over it! Stop trying to impose your misery on others by going around saying, 'Life is bad, life is horrible.' Life is tough on you? Well, boo hoo!

'Life is tough on you? Well, boo hoo!'

ANGLE ON THE AUDIENCE

... *laughing.*

ON VIDEO: EXT. LIVINGSTON HOME – DAY

Scooby talks to Toby in the backyard, Marty seen in the distant background.

SCOOBY
... Well, yeah, my Dad is kind of a goofball. I just have to pretend to go along with his ideas. 'Cause he really doesn't get it: like I could be the next Oprah, for all he knows, but he's never even seen the show.

ANGLE ON SCOOBY

... *watching himself on screen.*

ON VIDEO: NEW ANGLE ON SCOOBY

... *as he continues talking to Toby.*

                    TOBY (O.S.)
What is most important to you?

                    SCOOBY
I dunno. I'd like to be good at something. It doesn't have to
be TV. I mean, it could be movies . . . Anything. I'd be willing
to direct.

The audience laughs.

But I'd like to be, you know . . . famous. Not necessarily a
superstar, just famous. Be recognized. Get fan mail. Things . . .

ON VIDEO: TIGHTER ON SCOOBY

. . . still talking to Toby.

                    TOBY (O.S.)
Uh, Scooby, now I understand how you want to be a TV
talk-show host and all, like Conan O'Brien, but did you
know even *he* went to college?

                    SCOOBY
He did?

                    TOBY (O.S.)
Yeah. He went to Harvard.

                    SCOOBY
                    (*beat*)
Oh.

ANGLE ON SCOOBY

*. . . watching the film and listening to the audience. The laughter is out
of control. He is devastated.*

INT. LIVINGSTON HOME – NIGHT

Marty and Fern are in bed watching the news.

Mikey appears in the doorway.

                    MIKEY
Mom? Dad? Can I sleep with you? I'm scared.

They flick off the TV.

        MARTY

Sure! . . .

        FERN

Of course, honey. Come in bed with us. Come on.

Mikey gets in bed with them.

        MARTY

Snug as a bug in a rug. Yeah, here you go, pal. All righty . . . You're monster-proofed!

EXT. LIVINGSTON HOME – NIGHT

Consuelo approaches the house stealthily.

ANGLE ON FINGERS

. . . opening the back door of the house;

stuffing towels under bedroom doors;

turning on the kitchen stove's gas;

switching on the main gas valve in the boiler room.

EXT. LIVINGSTON HOME – NIGHT

Consuelo flees.

A very long pause.

    FADE TO BLACK.

EXT. STREET NEAR LIVINGSTON HOME – EARLY MORNING

Scooby gets off the bus with a few cleaning women. He walks homewards.

EXT. LIVINGSTON HOME – DAY

Scooby sees reporters, policemen, firemen, ambulances, gas company vehicles, and neighbors surrounding his house.

Toby's last interview with Scooby.

Toby and Mike suddenly appear with their camera trained on him.

ON VIDEO

> TOBY (O.S.)
> Oh, my God, Scooby! I'm so sorry . . . I'm so, so sorry . . .
>
> SCOOBY
> Don't be. Your movie's a hit.